# IT CHASED ME

STRANGE ENCOUNTERS

VOLUME 3

Compiled and edited by
Tom Lyons

IT CHASED ME: STRANGE ENCOUNTERS, VOLUME 3

Copyright © 2023 Tom Lyons

All rights reserved. No part of this may be reproduced without the author's prior consent, except for brief quotes used in reviews.

All information and opinions expressed in *It Chased Me: Strange Encounters, Volume 3,* are based upon the personal perspectives and experiences of those generous enough to submit them. Tom Lyons does not purport that the information presented in this book is based on accurate, current, or valid scientific knowledge.

## Acknowledgments

It's no easy task for people to discuss their encounters with cryptids. I want to thank the many good people who took the time and energy to put their experiences into writing.

Some of the following names were altered to protect people's privacy.

# Would you like to see your report in an issue of *It Chased Me: Strange Encounters*?

If so, all you have to do is type up a summary of your experience and email it to Tom Lyons at:

Living.Among.Bigfoot@gmail.com

## **Special Offer**

If you submit a report and it is accepted, you will receive an exclusive paperback copy signed by Tom shortly after the book is released. If you'd like to participate in that offer, please include your mailing address in the email.

# Contents

Report #1 ............................................................. 1
Report #2 ........................................................... 27
Report #3 ........................................................... 45
Report #4 ........................................................... 66
Conclusion ......................................................... 97
Editor's Note ..................................................... 99
Mailing List Sign-Up Form .............................. 101
Social Media .................................................... 103
About the Editor ............................................. 105

IT CHASED ME: STRANGE ENCOUNTERS, VOLUME 3

## Report #1

Hello. I've decided it's finally time to get a story of mine out into the open. I'm unsure how it took me so long to realize that I could share a typed summary while remaining anonymous. That's why I never discussed my experience with anyone other than my family and two closest friends. I hate to admit it, but I've always been afraid of being mocked, for I think very few people would find anything I have to say credible. So, before I forget, I want to quickly thank you, Tom, for compiling these reports. My daughter gifted me one of these books for my birthday a few months ago, and I must admit it made me feel a newfound sense of security and optimism for the future. It was pleasing to know so many people have shared startling experiences and have been completely fine ever since. Your books encouraged me to be more confident, so here I am.

In 1988, I had gone to pick up a pizza for my older brother's party. He had recently gotten hired as a firefighter in Malibu, California, and our family wanted to celebrate. The guy had been trying to get hired for well over a year after graduating from the fire Academy, and it seemed he just couldn't land a job anywhere. We had been feeling so bad for him, especially since he had a newborn baby on the way, which was this first one. I had always looked up to him for his hard work, so seeing him feeling insecure about how he would provide for his family felt so awkward. I know our parents would have helped him if the worst-case scenario had arrived, but my brother was extremely prideful, so everyone could tell that the worrying was eating him alive.

It was relieving to hear that my brother had gotten hired, but it was even better that he got a job in the next town over from where we all lived, which was Topanga, California. Everyone in our family had been bracing themselves for the day we would learn that my brother had to move to another state or even across the country, given it was nowhere near as easy to land a career as a firefighter as we had hoped. I'm unsure why, but I think we all assumed people were automatically assigned positions once they graduated from fire academies. That was far from the case, and boy, did we learn the hard way.

We were ecstatic that my brother had finally gotten hired and would be around while raising his first-born baby. My mother nearly had a heart attack from overwhelming joy when she learned the news. Everything felt perfect for the first time in a while, but things would change for me only hours later.

I was still in my last year of high school, so I didn't have much money to spend as I pleased, but I wanted to ensure I contributed to the festivities. Without telling anyone, I snuck into my car and drove to my brother's favorite local pizza place to pick up a couple of pies for everyone.

I kept my departure a secret because several family members would have demanded that they give me the money to pay for the food. But I was determined to do a nice thing by treating everyone. I didn't get many chances to do something like that back then, so I considered the situation the perfect opportunity to do a kind thing for my brother and the rest of my family. I was so proud of the guy and wanted to express that immediately.

The events occurred in February, so it was already dark when I snuck out to get the pizzas. If you are unfamiliar with the town of Topanga, try to envision A network of curvy, narrow roads surrounded by woods. It was a wonderful place to live, but driving around the area was rather treacherous, especially after sundown. After getting my driver's license, it took a lot of pleading for my parents to allow me to drive alone.

My high school was within walking distance, so there weren't many occasions when I needed to be behind the wheel solo. I remember feeling so liberated once they agreed to let me take a date to the movies, understanding that asking my crush to pick me up would be embarrassing. And there was no way I was willing to have my mother or father drop us up at the cinema.

I decided to take a series of side streets to have a better chance of avoiding delay. If you're familiar with that area, you probably know how congested traffic can get around or anywhere near Los Angeles. Having lived there since I was four, I knew the place like the back of my hand.

Therefore, I knew all the best secret routes. I distinctly remember blasting a Depeche Mode song on the radio as I whipped through those hilly streets. I was in such a good mood and couldn't wait to surprise my family with the pizza. They were all back home, enjoying cocktails, under the impression that I had gone to shower and clean up for the rest of the night. This all happened well before mobile phones were anywhere near as common as they are today, so nobody could contact me to check where I had gone, even if they wanted to.

I had never done anything like what I was doing before, so everything about that evening was exciting to my senses. Well, it wasn't long after I had turned onto one of the more secluded streets that I was met by a different type of excitement—one comprised of terror.

I'm unsure how to describe it other than to say that it suddenly looked like daytime. As if that wasn't confusing enough, I noticed that the light extended maybe fifty yards beyond the hood of my vehicle. I then looked in the rearview mirror and saw the luminescence covering the same distance behind me. *What the hell's going on?* I looked out my side windows and noticed the same thing to my right and left. Even more mysteriously, my car slowed down the moment things lit up, which was none of my doing. Another strange thing was that it didn't sound like the engine was dying; it was more like some outside force was responsible.

Eventually, my speed slowed two less than five miles per hour, and that was when I peeked my head out the window to see if I could see anything above me that might be causing everything. That was when I saw a dark triangular object matching my speed and making no noise I could hear over my vehicle's motor. The aircraft's appearance reminded me a lot of a stealth bomber, but I immediately knew it couldn't be because it must have been around a third of the size—probably less. It couldn't have been more than twenty feet above my car.

Not long after I spotted the aircraft, seemingly everything around me became transparent. That included my vehicle, the ground, and even the nearby trees. Nobody else was around, so I was unsure whether the transparency was available only to my eyes or if that was how everything would have looked to anyone nearby at that moment. That view must have lasted for about five seconds before everything started flickering back and forth between the transparency and how it all looked regularly. That was when I somehow regained control and intended to get away.

It might have been because I was approaching a lot of low-hanging tree cover, but I was under the impression that the small aircraft had left the area. I wondered what it was doing there and why it seemed so interested in me. Who was inside of it? What would they have wanted with such an average young man like myself? And why have they decided to leave the scene when they did? I was so shocked by the incident that it took me a minute or two to realize that I had made a couple of wrong turns after the aircraft vanished.

I felt it was a good idea to pull over and regather my senses, even though I knew it probably wasn't wise to make myself a sitting duck. However, I was so unnerved by the whole thing that I didn't feel like I had complete control over my body, and I desperately needed to take a breather. While looking for a place to pull over, I was happy to pass a couple of other vehicles appearing to be driving normally.

Immediately after I found a small side street, I parked my car while keeping the engine running. That was when I noticed how badly I was sweating. My drenched shirt made me feel like I had lost every ounce of water. I had to look in my rearview mirror a handful of times to establish that I was okay and very much still alive.

By the time I had calmed my heart rate a bit, all I could think about was how badly I wanted to know whether that aircraft was of human origin. It was so small then I realized it could even be some remote-controlled drone for all I knew. It didn't seem like there was enough space for a living, breathing pilot behind the steering wheel—if it even had one.

Eventually, I reached a point where I felt safe enough to peek my head out the driver-side window to check the sky above me. Initially, it appeared that nothing more than cloud cover obstructed the night sky, So I felt comfortable enough to step outside to stretch my arms and legs. I had been so stressed and tense that it felt like my entire body was on the verge of cramping up. It also could have been because I had become severely dehydrated.

But it wasn't long after I stepped onto the cracked asphalt that I turned around and saw something above my car. Whatever it was, it was maybe twelve feet above and appeared to be hovering. The only way I can think to describe what I saw was to say that it looked like how the monster appears in the movie *The Predator* when it uses a device that makes it almost invisible, but there's still a trace of movement. I apologize if you're unfamiliar with the film; I can't imagine anything else to compare it to. Such an awful feeling swept over me at that moment. I felt extremely trapped, especially considering the street I had parked on had no outlet, and my vehicle wasn't facing the preferred direction.

I had never felt so vulnerable at any point in my life before that moment, even though I knew zilch about the aircraft. I should clarify that as I slowly stepped toward my vehicle, I wasn't sure that the aircraft or anything that had to do with it was causing the strange visual. For all I knew at that moment, it could have been a byproduct of the trauma of the previous event or dehydration, causing me to see things I couldn't explain. But right after I sat back in the driver's seat and shut the door, I decided to take one last peek out the window.

That was when I received confirmation that it was the aircraft above my car. This time, it was entirely visible. My heart rate sped up, and everything around me, including my figure, became transparent. I could see all of my bones and what I assumed had to be on the network of veins running through my biological system.

Then, within what felt like a mere second, I next noticed that I was sitting at the kitchen table with my family. The sudden change of venue felt even stranger when I realized I was no longer sweating profusely. As far as I could tell, nothing was different about my appearance than when I had left to pick up the food.

"Where did these pizzas come from?" I asked, looking around at everyone, observing how they all seemed as normal and cheery as possible. I had to ask a second time, for I suppose I was too quiet the first time around.

"What do you mean?" my mother, who happened to be seated closest to me, said. "You brought them here."

I soon discovered that I had walked the pizzas through the front door a bit earlier, and nobody even thought I was acting strange until I asked where the pies had come from. I couldn't (and still don't) understand how I could have reentered our house in a typical, casual fashion. The last thing I remembered was feeling scared shitless.

I had no idea what to say to my family, for I didn't want to risk ruining their celebratory moods. I mean, would they have been able to believe anything of what I said happened to me anyway? It seemed best to wait until the festivities calmed down the next day or the day after before I shared my strange experience. Had I revealed any of it right then and there at the kitchen table, I'm sure it would have dampened the mood. They might've suspected I was on hardcore drugs. That skepticism would have ruined what should have been one of the highlights of my brother's life. It took a ton of discipline, but fortunately, I held back.

I think a lot of that was just because I didn't even know how to put what I had experienced into words. Honestly, what was I supposed to say? It was more than apparent that it wasn't the right time or place to talk about any of it, and it was probably beneficial for me to wait until I had some relaxing time alone to evaluate what might have happened to me during that drive to pick up pizza.

While lying in bed later that night, I thought it was odd how confident I felt that whatever I had encountered earlier had little to no interest in returning. Call me crazy, but it was almost as if I had had some interaction that I couldn't fully remember but had somehow given me the courage to continue my life normally. My subconscious remembered something, but I couldn't think of any specifics.

But aside from my emotions, I thought a lot about theories regarding the nature of the event. I'm sure many readers will insist I was visited by aliens of extraterrestrial origin, which very well might have been the case. But I lean more toward the idea that I was approached by simulation engineers, programmers, or whatever you prefer to call them.

Of course, that isn't to say that whoever controls the simulation isn't extraterrestrial, but the encounter forced me to look at our existence much differently. It wouldn't surprise me at all if I were to discover that we were immersed in some computer program. But if that is the case, what would that mean for the thing that we call the universe? Would it still have limits to its boundaries, or are we talking about something else entirely?

I'm unsure why, but I didn't get the impression that whoever controlled the small aircraft was hostile toward me. And there's always the possibility that that perspective is merely a coping mechanism. I prefer to think otherwise. I still get freaked out while thinking about it sometimes. There have even been occasions where the mere acknowledgment of what I experienced almost caused minor hallucinations. I wouldn't say they are visual, but everything around me starts to feel highly unfamiliar, and it's like I no longer even know who I am—or *what* I am. What are humans, and why are we here—wherever *here* is?

I have talked to my brother about what had happened more than anyone else in my family, for he has always been the most open-minded when it comes to questioning this existence and what else might occupy space. The subject of time has always been one of his favorites to discuss because he thinks that humans have it all wrong, though he doesn't claim to know the correct way of perceiving all of it. He didn't seem to agree with my outlook on everything that happened to me on that strange evening, but he has made it apparent that he believes my claim is sincere. Unfortunately, everyone else in my family has been pretty dismissive, whether they realize it or not.

It must be so difficult not to have anyone you're close with taking your rare and mysterious experiences seriously. I am lucky to have a brother who wasn't quick to rule out any possibilities and genuinely listened to what I had to say. I have a hunch that too many people don't have that and end up feeling very lonely after their unexplainable experiences. Therefore,

thank you for allowing me to vent
about what I underwent.

IT CHASED ME: STRANGE ENCOUNTERS, VOLUME 3

My New Podcast is available on Apple and Spotify

## Report #2

Hello there, I'm Nikki. I'm from the smaller Chicago suburb of Highland Park. I had a life-altering night about eight years ago while visiting home during my winter break from college. I've undergone many counseling sessions since and recently accepted that I'll likely never feel the same again. I've been told that that form of acceptance is a critical part of the recovery process and that it's best to work toward it as soon as possible.

Growing up in our big house was always a bit scary, especially since I was an only child. Aside from the occasional sleepover with a friend, I never had anyone to commiserate with me on how frightening our mansion became after dark. And the fear wasn't exclusive to nighttime. There were plenty of occasions when I was home alone and wouldn't go near certain parts of the house that didn't get plenty of natural light. Only one family owned our house before my parents purchased it when I was just a baby, and they always assured me that they didn't have a grim history.

But it wasn't just the possibility of ghosts or monsters lurking inside our house and around our property. It was also the notion that there were plenty of rooms throughout where a psychopathic intruder could be awaiting a perfect opportunity to strike.

So, my body had always had an undesirable habit of needing to pee in the middle of the night, which meant I had to navigate my way through the dark to get to the bathroom. You probably think I could have saved myself from the terror by turning on the lights before exiting my bedroom; however, the closest bathroom was a considerable way down the hallway, and there was no nearby light switch to illuminate the path. Explaining without showing a blueprint of the floor plan is difficult, so you'll have to take my word for it.

In any case, my dad was hell-bent on preserving energy, so he always ensured the lights were off in the areas nobody was using. I believe my grandfather created his obsessive-compulsive disorder. They didn't have nearly as much money while my dad was growing up, and my grandparents looked to save every penny whenever possible. Stories about my father's upbringing have always made me slightly sad, so I did my best to work with him rather than protest every little thing that didn't make sense to me. I recall nagging my dad to leave the lights on a few times when I was a little kid, but I gave up at a pretty early age. He had always been so kind and understanding in every other aspect, so I didn't want to give him too hard of a time.

During my teenage years, I started to get this awful feeling whenever I went to the bathroom in the middle of the night. I couldn't help but sense that someone was watching me. I had told my parents about it in the past, but they would always brush it off. My mom claimed she had similar feelings whenever she would get up in the middle of the night for anything. But according to her, it was nothing to worry about.

I had that unnerving feeling for years before the night of the incident, which undoubtedly made the whole experience even creepier. I hated how it confirmed that I wasn't being overly paranoid or acting crazy whenever I sensed there were eyes on me in the dark. I always left the bathroom door ajar whenever I had to relieve myself, for I knew there was no chance either of my parents would visit that area in the middle of the night. A bit of moonlight pierced through small windows in the nearby hallway, so I wanted to use that.

I'll never forget when I was sitting on the toilet, looking toward my toes, when I noticed a figure run past the doorway. Whatever it was, it was low to the ground, and I would have assumed it was our dog—if we had ever had one. I so badly wished for any way I could justify the notion that my eyes had played tricks on me. But I saw enough to know that that was not the case.

Whatever had run past the doorframe was still out there, for I could hear its footsteps that were much more like fast-paced taps than humanlike footsteps. It sounded like whatever was causing them couldn't weigh much. I had no idea what could've been lurking in that hallway; all I knew was that my worst nightmare had come true.

"Dad?" I attempted to call out a few times, but each try was too soft and quiet. The fear caused my body to tense, causing me to lose total control. Soon after the tapping faded, I assumed that whatever I saw in the hallway had gone to a different section of the house. After a few silent moments of thinking the coast was clear, I got off the toilet, pulled my shorts back up, and rushed toward the exit. I had planned to run straight for my parents' branch of the house, but the bathroom door suddenly slammed shut, seemingly on its own.

All I could think to do then was to power on the bathroom light before I even attempted to exit again. That was when I heard the raspy breaths behind me. I've never felt my body freeze up as severely as it did during those moments. I had enough control to turn my head slightly, and I could see the dark human-sized silhouette standing in the bathtub. Its body appeared to be twitching violently, almost like it was convulsing.

I can't emphasize enough how glad I am that I didn't possess the ability to entirely turn my head and lock eyes with whatever stood behind me. I feel that if I had seen its face, the visual would've engrained itself into my mind. I probably would've spent the rest of my days seeing it in the most random of places. Still, I could see enough out of my peripheral view to watch the figure quickly rise toward the feeling, latch onto it, and begin crawling in my direction. By the way, I don't know whether it floated to the ceiling or leaped like an animal.

That was when I lost it, and my muscles seemed to take control of themselves. Screaming as loud as possible, I ripped the door open and ran down the hall toward my parents' room. I was so glad when I noticed the lights in their hallway powered on, for I knew they had heard the commotion and were on their way to me.

To my surprise, my mom was the first to appear, running around the corner. I could tell that something behind me caught her attention, causing me to worry that we were all about to be attacked. However, her gaze quickly shifted to me, and she kept moving forward. My dad followed closely behind.

After arriving in their arms, I looked over my shoulder and saw nothing other than the usual hallway decor. "Where is it? Where did it go?" I muttered repeatedly, my heart feeling like it was about to leap out of my chest.

"What? Where did *what* go?" my parents kept asking, but I didn't even know how to respond other than to say, "It was there! I saw it!"

"Honey, it's okay," my parents started interrupting my panic-induced ranting. "There's nothing there. You must've had a nightmare."

"This was no dream! Mom, I know you saw it when you entered the hallway. I know you did!" I argued as tears flowed down my cheeks. "We need to call the police!"

I watched my dad glance at my mom in a way that requested reassurance that she hadn't seen anyone or anything.

Mom shook her head without vocally replying to my dad. I sensed she had convinced herself that her eyes must've played tricks on her while she was still waking up. Although it frustrated me that both of my parents claimed I must've imagined the frightening scenario, it was nice to know that I was no longer being chased.

I slept in my parents' bathroom for the next handful of nights. It got to the point where, although still scared, I concluded that the previous experience was just a one-time occurrence. Regardless of how I became comfortable enough to sleep in my room again, I knew that whatever had approached me was inhuman—at least, in its current state.

I've spoken to a few spiritual professionals over the years, and they all explained that what I saw was a physical manifestation of negative energy, to put it in a nutshell. They claim there is a lot more to it than that, but the bulk of it is beyond my understanding, and I'll likely mess it up if I even attempt to explain any of it.

I never even tried super hard to comprehend it because I was more concerned about the likelihood of whether it would return. The experts also reassured me that even if I were to reencounter it, it wouldn't be able to harm me in the ways that I feared. I can't say whether that was accurate, but I desperately wanted to believe they knew what they were talking about. That required a lot of faith.

I've never fully mentally recovered since that night, and I always make sure to have a cross nearby, no matter where I go, even if it's in necklace form. I must admit that that makes me feel an added sense of security, even though I'm convinced that the dark entity has no reason to chase me again.

I believe my frightening experience gave me some wisdom I wouldn't have acquired from any other means, for it opened my mind to what's possible in our strange world. It also helped me to feel a lot more compassion and empathy toward those who have undergone terrifying experiences of their own, only to have the majority of society dismiss and even ridicule their claims. I find it pitiful when people mock others for trying to be honest about strange things that happen to them. Believe me when I say it's not easy to come up with the words to describe the circumstances. I have a much easier time talking about it now, but it took me a considerably long time to reach that point, and I don't think that that struggle receives the attention it deserves.

I was a bit upset with my parents for quite some time, but simultaneously grateful that they were home during my encounter. Who knows what might have happened to me had I been alone when that mysterious entity visited my home? As I'm sure you can understand, I don't like to put too much thought into that. But I also think it's worth acknowledging that that happens to too many innocent people.

These types of encounters must be why some go missing and are never heard from again.

To claim your free eBook, visit
www.LivingAmongBigfoot.com
and click the FREE BOOKS tab!

## Report #3

I'll start by mentioning I'm a simple man who has lived in Bandera, Texas, my whole life and never thought much about the world of cryptozoology until dealing with a rare animal a few years back.

In the summer of 2021, my sheep started vanishing from my ranch. It got to a point where it happened weekly, and I can't begin to tell you how much it stumped me. I knew it couldn't be wolves or coyotes, for there would've been visible blood trails. There were even times when I wondered if I was going insane, for there was a long period where there was no evidence that I even had the number of sheep I thought I had in the first place. That was an unsettling feeling. My parents raised me on that property, and we had never dealt with anything anywhere near as unusual. Since there was a history of dementia stemming from my mother's side of the family tree, the now regular-occurring confusion caused me to speculate whether my brain was in for some serious trouble.

Alzheimer's had always been the most intimidating disease, as far as I was concerned, so I was having a progressively more difficult time after each disappearance. To make matters worse, I was reluctant to ask any of my neighbors or other community members if they had noticed any differences in my behavior. I have never been the most social person, so most of my interaction with others came from supermarket employees, hardware store employees, and others who occasionally assisted me at the ranch. And, for whatever reason, I felt insecure about those individuals suspecting I could be on the verge of losing my marbles. Now I believe that most of that fear stemmed from my family's history of dementia. I was taught from an early age that it was one of the worst things that could happen to someone.

I must've lost four or five sheep by the time I heard my horse, Margo, making all sorts of commotion. She was an extremely relaxed, confident horse that seldom lost her cool. The only other instance where I can recall her losing her cool was when a diesel engine-powered truck had to get inside her enclosure to remove the pieces of an old shed I had meant to get rid of for years. So, when I heard Margo panicking, I immediately knew something strange was happening outside.

It was around 1:30 in the morning when the noise woke me, and the first thing I did after jumping out of bed was run to get my rifle. I don't think there's ever been another time when I felt so determined to fix a situation. Although I didn't understand what was happening, my intuition told me that whatever spooked my horse was the same thing responsible for stealing my sheep. I'm not trying to brag by mentioning this, but I wouldn't even say I was all that scared of whatever was out there. I was much more frightened of the culprit getting away with taking another sheep or, worse, harming Margo.

With a flashlight in one hand and my rifle in the other, I opened my side door as carefully as possible. That was the only door in my house that didn't slam shut automatically, enabling my best chance of arriving at the scene undetected. I could still hear my horse trotting around and neighing with distress, leading me to believe that whatever had spooked her was still in sight and romping around the property.

I first checked on the sheep, figuring they were much more vulnerable. They were all huddled together, having likely heard Margo's warning. Luckily, their numbers hadn't depleted any further. That was when I became genuinely worried for my horse, still making noise in the distance. Before that moment, I had still been ignorant, deciding that there were no predators in that region large enough to consider going after a healthy horse—especially one as big as Margo.

But an awful feeling came over me as I rushed toward the horse's stable. I started thinking about how there are said to be more tigers in captivity within the state of Texas than currently in the wild. Believe it or not, that's a legitimate fact. Supposedly, it's not all that difficult to get your hands on tiger cubs if you know someone who knows someone. Texas and other southern states have a relatively big black market for tiger cubs and other exotic animals. I started thinking about how that's a reality I hadn't taken as seriously as I probably should've and that there might very well be a tiger attacking my horse at that very moment.

So, not only had I become worried over my horse, but I was also second-guessing whether I had enough firepower to take down a hungry adult tiger. The situation started feeling much more out of my control than before—like I could be running toward my death. Still, I wasn't about to give up. That horse meant the world to me. I had had her for years and formed a strong bond. I much preferred her company over the company of people.

It's quite impressive how many emotions rose to the surface as I ran toward my horse stable. I had never before experienced what was so obviously the notorious 'fight-or-flight' mode. I wasn't about to let anything kill and eat Margo, no matter the severity of injuries I might endure.

Once I had made it within fifty or sixty yards of the fence, I saw the beast slowly circling my horse—but I could immediately tell it was no tiger. It was about a quarter of Margo's size, moved on all fours, and had pointy batlike ears. After getting a little closer, I spotted a long wispy tail—a lot like an opossum's.

Although I almost couldn't believe what I was looking at, I was far more concerned with my horse, who, fortunately, didn't appear to have any injuries. I sensed I had gotten there in the nick of time, but I was still too far away to get an accurate shot at the beast. Given my current angle, the risk of hitting my horse was too significant. Without further delay, I fired a warning shot into the sky, immediately capturing the unidentified creature's attention. But the beast didn't flee. Instead, it crouched onto the ground, making it look more like it was about to pounce rather than run off. It made a soft but odd-sounding snarl.

Before long, I was within fifteen yards of the strange animal, and that was when I noticed its red glowing eyes. At a close distance, this thing looked like a demon straight out of hell. I'm convinced something about its appearance made me feel awful, not just afraid. I've never believed in all that woo-woo voodoo crap, but I genuinely think being near this thing had a strange effect on my body. Maybe it had something to do with pheromones. I have no idea. All I know is that there was *something* to it.

The only reasons I wanted to continue approaching the strange animal were to obtain a more advantageous shot and to get a handle on what it was. I doubt I would've gotten closer if it had not been near my horse. But my instincts told me it would be lights out for Margo unless I intervened. But with every step I took toward the thing, I felt exponentially more in danger.

Once I was within maybe twelve yards of the beast, it displayed what was between its jaws. That was when I saw the pair of fangs that reminded me of what you see on a vampire bat, only much longer. I should've pulled the trigger while the creature stood still, but I suppose I was too stunned by the sight of the thing, causing my reactions to delay. The beast then started pacing back and forth like big cats sometimes do inside their zoo enclosures. It didn't take its eyes off me, and that's when I knew I was in significant trouble.

The speed of its pacing increased to the point where I didn't know what to do other than fire another shot into the air. But all that seemed to do was anger the creature. It ceased its pacing before reentering a crouched position and stepping toward me. Terrified, I fired another warning shot, but the beast didn't stop creeping toward me. The most intense fear came over me, and I turned to start running for my house.

I figured it was only moments before I would feel fangs and claws penetrate the back of my skull, but I somehow managed to make it into my house. I looked over my shoulder and saw the creature progressing toward me while repeatedly looking back at my horse. I had the impression that it was having trouble deciding who to go after.

After slamming the door shut behind me, I looked through the window and saw no sign of the unidentified predator. Once I felt safer, all I could think about was Margo. But I couldn't hear her making any additional noise. I knew I needed to get back out there to check on her, but I decided first to call the police. I had preferred not to involve authorities of the law in my life, but I didn't think I had much of a choice anymore. I knew doing so would lead to the best chances of rescuing my horse from severe injuries and potential death.

The 9-1-1 dispatcher didn't say much other than they were sending someone to help me. They didn't even seem all that fazed when I told them that a large unknown predator had stolen several sheep and was now stalking my horse. They maintained a monotone throughout our brief conversation before requesting I remain inside until assistance arrived.

A police car pulled onto my property only a few minutes later, so there must've already been an officer in my general area when I made the call. That was pretty lucky, for I don't believe there are all that many local officers due to the town's small population.

I left my rifle inside when I went outside to greet the man and quickly explain the situation. I was surprised when he informed me that his department had received several calls about a strange "wolf-like" animal snooping around local people's properties. Therefore, the officer didn't act like I could be delusional or anything like that. I could tell he was confident that there must be *something* strange and rare lurking nearby. He even permitted me to grab my rifle before the two of us went to check up on the horse stable. I appreciated how he trusted me enough to do that. He might've been a little scared, himself.

I can't express how glad I was to find Margo still alive. Even better, she still didn't appear to have any injuries. I was so worried that the lack of noise indicated that she was in deep trouble, and sometimes I wonder if she had a guardian Angel looking out for her. The creature was nowhere in sight, so the police officer proceeded to check on the sheep—and that's when I realized that another was missing.

"Son of a bitch!" I grunted. Weirdly, it almost felt like the beast had planned the order of the events. But that's probably getting a little ridiculous. Anyhow, the officer gave his condolences regarding my missing sheep. He said he wished they could go after the creature that night since it could still be nearby, but the search would need to wait until sunrise. He didn't specify why that was, but he probably thought they had too few resources, and the situation would turn into a wild goose chase in the middle of the night.

Although I desperately wanted to find the bastard of an animal, I couldn't disagree with the guy. And after seeing what I saw inside my horse's stable, I wasn't about to explore the dark woods where the thing could be hiding behind any tree, waiting to pounce. It was easy to tell that the creature possessed incredible speed and agility. Attacking a person in the forest after sundown would probably be the equivalent of shooting fish in a barrel. I would practically be handing myself over on a silver platter.

Before the officer left, he and I discussed what the animal might be.

That was when he mentioned another local referred to it as a chupacabra. I immediately thought it was one of the goofiest words I had ever heard, and it took me a few attempts to figure out how to pronounce it correctly.

Police vehicles returned bright and early the following day, and they asked me to remain inside while they executed their search, which I must admit I was okay with. Additional unmarked vehicles drove onto my property, which indicated the authorities were taking the investigation very seriously.

I was pleased that someone was handling the situation and keeping my remaining animals safe. However, I didn't appreciate the lack of explanation when several authorities dragged a large body bag into a U-Haul-like truck. That was when it became clear that someone intended to keep the apprehended creature under wraps. The whole situation came to an end shortly after. There was nothing I could do to get an answer out of anyone.

I'll forever wonder what that strange animal was, but I would be willing to bet a pretty penny that it was a legendary chupacabra. I've never seen anything like it since.

# Visit My Digital Book Store

If you're looking for NEW reads, check out my digital store, www.TomLyonsBooks.com.

Buying my books directly from me means you save money—because my store will always sell for less than big retailers. My store also offers sales, deals, bundles, and pre-order discounts you won't find anywhere else.

## Report #4

Hi Tom, my name is Maura. I've meant to email you for a long time, so I hope this message finds you well and my story makes it into one of your publications. I'll start by thanking you for giving people a place to share their disturbing stories with the world. As you know quite well, given what you went through in your *Living Among*

*Bigfoot* book series, finding the right place to vent about these kinds of experiences is critical for sustaining mental health. So, again, thank you.

When I was in my early twenties, I was dating a guy named Trevor, who was an avid outdoorsman. When the weather was nice, one of his favorite things to do was take us to his family's lakeside cabin in Blue Hill, Maine. Trevor was the type who would get easily stressed about life, so enjoying that tranquil area was soothing for his racing mind.

There was one particular weekend when he was there with his family, and he returned to our hometown of Springfield, Massachusetts, somewhat spooked. He looked and acted like he had seen a ghost but was also excited to have found something rare. I didn't know what to think when he explained that he had witnessed a cloaked individual glide over his lake on their way into the woods.

Although I wasn't sure I could buy every word he told me, I knew he had to have seen *something* strange. He wasn't the type to make up stories or even embellish anything, so I knew he was at least sincere in believing whatever he thought he saw. In any case, he didn't seem to feel that it was dangerous, so he practically begged me to join him out there that following weekend so I could experience it for myself, whatever that meant.

I remember arguing with him about how slim the chances were that I would see the same thing if he saw something out of the ordinary. Honestly, I didn't want to experience what had made him feel the way he came off while telling me about it. I never really believed in aliens, ghosts, the abominable snowman, etc., but I wasn't one to go looking for them either. I didn't want to risk encountering them even though I saw it as a less than 1% chance I would. It was weirdly important to him that I joined him on his little adventure, so I gave in. That would become the worst decision of my life.

It was cool and rainy when we arrived at the cabin, so I expected not to spend much time outside. But by that point, Trevor wasn't willing to let anything get in the way of our investigation of the phenomenon. I quickly began expressing interest in going inside and watching a movie, but it was useless. He wouldn't have it. He wanted to remain hanging out on this little lot of ground beside the lake where there was a hammock, a couple of chairs, and a tarp he secured above our heads. There was also plenty of tree cover over there, so Trevor had decided it was the most advantageous location to watch for something that probably didn't want to be found.

The longer that time went on, the more delusional my ex seemed. It might have been the combination of feeling cold and bored, but I remember that being the first time I questioned whether we were a good match. Trevor's personality had begun to feel so different out of nowhere, and with each passing day during the previous week, I questioned more and more if he would remain like that. He was so different than before, and I had trouble understanding it. I couldn't relate at all. He had never acted like this at any point in our relationship. In some ways, it had begun to feel like I was interacting with an eager small child rather than what had been a masculine young man.

There were numerous occasions when we had been sitting in the hammock relaxing, and suddenly, Trevor would burst from our position and drag me by my hand to get a closer look at the lake. It was very uncomfortable each time that happened. It was weird how his sites always seemed to be on the sky above the water, further insinuating that he thought he had seen something remarkable.

Finally, after what had to be close to three hours, Trevor informed me that it was okay for us to go inside. I was so grateful and convinced him to join me for a warm bubble bath. His agreeing to that was like music to my ears, and I ran to open one of the expensive bottles of wine we had purchased on the way to the cabin.

What had been a relatively cold and miserable day soon felt like a warm and romantic evening.

Shortly after entering the hot bathtub, all those slight feelings of detachment quickly faded. I began to feel so pleased that we had planned the trip in the first place, and I even experienced a closeness to Trevor that I hadn't for quite some time. But thinking back on that now, I'm unsure whether that was anything more than the wine talking.

I'll never forget how my heart felt when a loud knock on the door suddenly interrupted our conversation. It didn't make sense that somebody would be there at that time. That lake was extremely isolated, and there weren't even any neighbors in sight aside from maybe one other small cabin across the water. Even if Trevor's parents had suddenly decided to join us without notice, they were too calm and cool to bang on the door like that. That wasn't in their nature.

Before I could even whisper a word to Trevor, he did something similar to what he had done multiple times on the hammock earlier. He jumped out of the tub, causing me to fall forward and drop my half-full wine glass into the water. I immediately thought it was so strange that he ran out of the bathroom completely nude and wet with suds all over him.

Even if there was an aggressive intruder, and he wanted to intercept them before they could cause us any harm, it seemed pretty ridiculous that he wouldn't at least wrap a towel around his waist before confronting them. He also could've grabbed his pants lying on the bathroom floor. I mean, what was he going to do? Fight someone while naked? Then I began wondering whether he was expecting a visitor he hadn't told me about. But that wasn't like Trevor, for aside from me, he mostly preferred to be left alone. I couldn't think of anyone he would have invited to the cabin, especially without notifying me first.

As I raced to dry myself off, I tried to be as quiet as possible so that

I could listen for any indication of what was going on outside the bathroom. But the front door was a good distance from the restroom, making it seem even creepier that someone would have banged on it loud enough for us to hear it. Strangely, there was no noise of any kind. The environment was eerily quiet.

"Trevor?" I called out several times, but there was no answer. After putting on my clothes, I peeked out the bathroom door and still saw no signs of Trevor other than the soaked footprints he left behind on the wooden floor. After waiting a few minutes with the ominous silence, I started to get very scared—so scared that I tiptoed down the hallway, desperate for reassurance that my ex-boyfriend was okay and there was nothing to worry about. By that point, I had hoped I would find Trevor on the front patio, giving some innocent, lost individual directions to get to wherever they were going. But that wasn't the case.

I followed wet footprints to the ajar door and again found nothing but silence. Standing on the doormat, I called out my boyfriend's name. After shouting a warning about how upset I would be if he played some sort of cruel joke on me and again receiving no response, I ran back inside to put my shoes on. I wanted to ensure I was ready in case of an emergency and I needed to flee.

I nearly had a heart attack when Trevor suddenly appeared at the doorway. I hadn't heard him coming, and he was still nude but didn't seem in any way concerned about it.

"Oh my god," I gasped. "What happened to you? Who was at the door?"

Trevor didn't answer. Instead, he grabbed me by my hand and guided me outside, as eager as ever. I kept looking for anyone else who would explain the knock at the door, but I saw nothing other than trees on the way to the water.

"What are you doing? Where are you taking me?" I begged, but he wouldn't answer. It seemed he wasn't hearing me.

"Don't you want to put your pants on?" Had it not been for the ongoing mysterious circumstance, I might've assumed we were about to go skinny dipping, but my instincts told me something else was on my ex's mind.

Soon, we arrived at the shore, and I was stunned by the brightness of the stars. I had never seen them so vibrant and beautiful, and it quickly seemed like that was why he had brought me out there. It's bizarre that I had started to relax even though I hadn't figured out who had banged on the door. It was almost like I had been drugged by something far more influential than alcohol, and I was nowhere near as concerned as I should've been.

I had almost forgotten how weirdly silent everything was, or I didn't care, but a strange noise behind us suddenly reminded me.

"What is that?" I asked Trevor, but all he did was smile at me. It sounded kind of like a parrot cawing softly. The noise was so quiet that it took me a few listens to realize it was coming from behind us.

When I looked over my shoulder, I saw a cloaked figure standing about thirty feet away. I didn't feel nearly as afraid as I should've. Although nervous and confused, the confusion came more from wondering what *she* wanted with

Trevor and me. Yes, I suddenly knew without question that the cloaked figure was a she, which I still can't explain. It was as if the dimly lit figure was somehow familiar to me. Honestly, explaining most of this scenario is akin to describing the details of a dream, so I'm trying to be careful as I write it all down.

The cloaked woman approached us with a few slow steps before awkwardly hobbling toward us at a quicker speed. Then she returned to the slower, more cautious-looking pace. That pattern repeated until the cloaked figure was within five or six feet of us. Mysteriously, I didn't even feel the need to run away once she was close enough to where I could hear what sounded like she was sniffing us. I couldn't be sure since the cloak concealed her face, but I was pretty sure she was smelling something. Whatever it was, she seemed much more interested in doing it to me than Trevor. It was apparent she was already acquainted with my ex-boyfriend.

Then, out of nowhere, my brain unlocked itself from the full extent of what I assumed was hypnosis and quickly raced to decide the best course of action. It was as if I had two internal voices engaged in a tug of war, attempting to establish whether it was wise to run at that moment. By that point, the cloaked figure had slowly circled Trevor and me multiple times, presumably also trying to establish what to do with us. Soon, my senses started to return at full force, and I started eyeing the surrounding soil for anything I could utilize against the creepy stranger.

As soon as I managed to break free from the mental shackles, an odd sulfur-like odor traveled up my nostrils. I immediately knew it came from what I had already perceived as a sinister individual. I'm unsure how to put it other than to say it stunk like evil—if that's even a thing. I don't believe you would ever find this kind of smell coming from someone or something absent of a psychopathic mind.

"Trevor, RUN!" I shouted as the cloaked individual's head began extending toward mine, revealing a wrinkly face that looked more like what we've seen on traditional sketches of aliens rather than an older woman. I'll never forget how its neck protruded at a much longer length than any human is capable of. That alone was one of the most disturbing things I had ever seen. It was almost like a reptile's neck, as wild as that sounds.

After taking off, I glanced over my shoulder and found Trevor hadn't moved a muscle. If I remember correctly, he wasn't even looking at me, seemingly the least bit concerned that I had fled. Initially, the cloaked figure didn't seem interested in pursuing me. But after I had returned to the front patio, I glanced over my shoulder again and saw her flying toward me somewhat slowly. That was the moment when I confirmed everything my ex-boyfriend had told me was true.

I slammed the door shut before running to find the landline telephone. I located one in the kitchen, which was convenient because I simultaneously grabbed the first knife inside. Having punched the nine key, the one key, and another one key, I stood there trembling, anxiously awaiting the emergency operator's voice and the sounds of the front door opening. But there were neither. I then realized that there wasn't even a dial tone.

Suddenly, I noticed nothing other than that same eerie silence I had experienced not long before encountering the cloaked figure. After a few moments of failing to hear anyone or anything, I began rotating my gaze in search of activity outside the nearby windows. Given what I had seen from the cloaked figure, I couldn't trust that it would be impossible for her to make her way inside without using doors. Clearly, she had abilities beyond my understanding, so I couldn't rule out the possibility that she could teleport inside or something like that.

I vividly recall the sensation of the knife shaking in my hand, causing me to wonder if I would even be able to hold on to it if the cloaked figure were to approach me again. Although she was nowhere in sight, I had become much more terrified than when she sniffed us from mere feet away while circling us. That speaks volumes about how I had to be under the influence of some supernatural force before somehow breaking free from it.

As I continued scanning my surroundings, a familiar face abruptly appeared behind one of the windows. It was Trevor, but he didn't look like his usual self. His eyes were completely white as if they had rolled into the back of his head. Also, I'm almost positive I saw something moving around within his gaping mouth, but I could only withstand a glimpse before turning and running out of the kitchen.

I was about to head down the hallway recklessly, but then I noticed Trevor's car keys hanging from a hook near the front door. That was when I realized it might be one of those 'now-or-never' opportunities. I could see from my peripheral vision that Trevor was still standing outside the same window I had seen him previously, which was at the back of the house. Therefore, it was best to take advantage of the chance of there being only one crazy individual to intercept me on the way to the car.

I wasn't sure Trevor would have tried to prevent me from leaving, but his demonic-looking eyes informed me that it wasn't worth waiting for him to make a move. I felt he must be under the control of the cloaked figure, so I wanted to avoid both of them at all costs. Attempting to suppress my nerves, I dashed over to the car keys, shelved them in my pocket, glanced through one of the front windows, and noticed the coast appeared clear.

Having taken a deep breath, I ripped open the door and sprinted toward Trevor's car. Fortunately, nothing intercepted me before I entered the already unlocked doors. It almost felt too good to be true when the engine started without delay. I had probably convinced myself that the close figure would have somehow disabled the vehicle so nobody could leave the property unless she permitted it.

Not long after I started driving away, I looked in the rearview mirror and saw the cloaked figure. Strangely, she was running toward me instead of flying. I can't think of any reason why she would have chosen the slower and more exhausting form of travel. That's another aspect that will never make any sense. The only slight possibility I can come up with is that the whole thing was merely an intimidation tactic to get me out of there so that she could have Trevor to herself. If that happened to have been the case, she certainly was successful.

I'll never forget how the cloak figure's neck extended to a length of at least three feet after she stopped running. Who knows why she would have even done that other than to traumatize me? If she wasn't human, what on God's green earth was she? Had it not been for the long neck and the alien-like face, I would have 100% guessed that she was a witch or sorcerer. Everyone knows there are plenty of stories about real-life witches throughout the various ages, so I would have assumed I just had another one to add to the list of tallies. Of course, I can't be sure, but my instincts tell me that the cloaked figure was something else, even though I can't come up with a likely theory.

I didn't even bother telling the police what had happened, as I was smart enough to know they would never believe me. It seemed like all it would do was create problems for me. What I did do was call Trevor's parents as soon as I returned home. Unfortunately, they also seemed to think I was crazy because I probably did some hysterical acts after an argument with my boyfriend. They were irritated that I took his car and left him there. I dropped off his vehicle at their house that night but refrained from speaking to them in person.

I wouldn't be surprised if Trevor's parents suspected I had caught their son with another woman and was experiencing the raw emotional aftermath when I called them. But let me tell you, it was far different than whatever the hell they envisioned.

Coincidentally, Trevor's parents contacted me less than a week later. They claimed that their son wasn't acting like himself. Initially, they assumed it had something to do with our presumed arguments, but then his mother witnessed him doing something I'm not comfortable enough to mention. It was clear to her that something was off—very off. She begged me for advice, but I explained that my instincts nagged me to disengage with my ex. I had this weird feeling that I got let off the hook, and the last thing I wanted to do was somehow reverse that.

I had hoped I would one day receive an update on Trevor, informing me that he had returned to his normal state and wanted to fill me in on everything that had happened to him. Unfortunately, that day never came, and I never saw my ex-boyfriend again. To be truthful, I haven't even looked into what he's doing these days. He could be dead for all I know. His status is something I would rather stay in the dark about, for I fear the worst.

Thank you for taking the time out of your day to read my story.

IT CHASED ME: STRANGE ENCOUNTERS, VOLUME 3

## Conclusion

Thanks for reading! If you want more scary stories, read *Camping Horror Stories.*

# IT CHASED ME: STRANGE ENCOUNTERS, VOLUME 3

## Editor's Note

Before you go, I'd like to say "thank you" for purchasing this book.

I know you had various cryptid-related books to choose from, but you took a chance at my content.
Therefore, thanks for reading this one and sticking with it to the last page.

At this point, I'd like to ask you for a *tiny* favor; it would mean the world if you could leave a review wherever you purchased this book.

Your feedback will aid me in creating products you and many others can enjoy.

IT CHASED ME: STRANGE ENCOUNTERS, VOLUME 3

IT CHASED ME: STRANGE ENCOUNTERS, VOLUME 3

## Mailing List Sign-Up Form

Don't forget to sign up for the newsletter email list. I promise I will not use it to spam you but to ensure you always receive the first word on any new releases, discounts, or giveaways! All you need to do is visit the following URL and enter your email address.

URL-

http://eepurl.com/dhnspT

# IT CHASED ME: STRANGE ENCOUNTERS, VOLUME 3

## Social Media

Feel free to follow/reach out to me with questions or concerns on either Instagram or Twitter! I will do my best to follow back and respond to all comments.

**Instagram:**

@living_among_bigfoot

**Twitter:**

@AmongBigfoot

# IT CHASED ME: STRANGE ENCOUNTERS, VOLUME 3

## About the Editor

A simple man at heart, Tom Lyons lived an ordinary existence for his first 52 years. Native to the great state of Wisconsin, he went through the motions of everyday life, residing near his family and developing a successful online business. The world he once knew would completely change shortly after moving out west, where he was confronted by the allegedly mythical species known as Bigfoot.

You can email him directly at:

Living.Among.Bigfoot@gmail.com

Printed in Great Britain
by Amazon